IHS

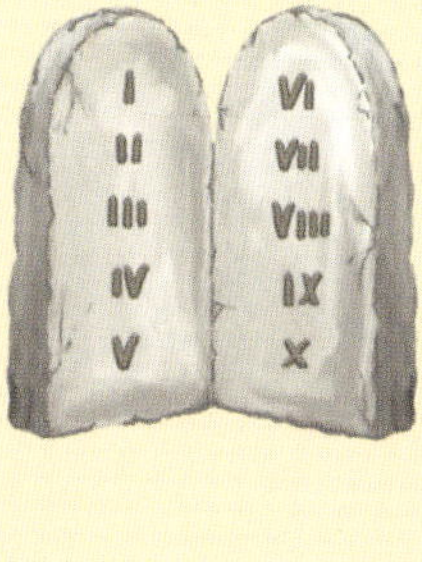
I
II
III
IV
V
VI
VII
VIII
IX
X

IHS
I
II
III
IV
V
VI
VII
VIII
IX
X

I BELIEVE

The Apostles' Creed for Little Catholics

By Sister M. Juliana of Maryknoll
Edited by Bart Tesoriero

ISBN: 978-1-61796-398-8

Printed in China

I believe in God.

God made me. He made me a person. He calls me by name. I am not like a dog or cat. They cannot draw pictures. They cannot tell stories. They cannot think about God. But I can because I am a person. I believe in God, even though I do not see Him. That is why God is so pleased to have me say, "I believe in You, dear God."

I believe in God.

I cannot see God, but I know Him, and I know that He loves me. He is everywhere, all around me. His ear is always close to my lips, so I can whisper little secrets to Him. If I am good, I shall see Him in heaven someday.

I believe in God the Father.

God wants us to know that He is our Father. He gives us everything we need. He takes good care of us.

God does not always give us everything we would like, because He does not want us to grow up spoiled and bad. He loves us too much for that. We should love everybody because God loves us all.

I believe in God, the Father Almighty.

God can do everything. He can give us brothers and sisters. He can take people away to heaven, when it is time for them to die. He holds the whole world in His hands. But there are some things God cannot do. He cannot be mean, or tell lies, or cheat.

I believe in God, the Father Almighty, Creator of Heaven.

God made hundreds and thousands of strong, bright angels. He gave them a nice place called heaven to live in. Heaven is to be our home, too, if we are good and love God. The angels were good when God made them, but some of them turned bad. We call the bad ones devils.

I believe in God, the Father Almighty, Creator of heaven and earth.

God made the beautiful world all for us. He made Adam to be the first father of all the people in the world. He made Eve to be Adam's wife. God told Adam and Eve that if they obeyed what He told them, they would never be sick or unhappy and they would never die. Some day they would go to heaven to be with God and the angels.

But Adam and Eve did not obey God. So heaven's door was shut. They could not get in. None of their children could get in, either.

I believe...
in Jesus Christ.

I believe...
in Jesus Christ, His only Son,
Our Lord.

After Adam's sin, sickness and death came upon all people. Sadness and sin had made a great change. But God already had a plan. He had chosen to send His Son to save us, so we would not be lost. The name of God's Son is Jesus Christ.

God

I believe…
in Jesus Christ, His only Son, Our Lord, who was conceived by the Holy Spirit.

There is only one God, but there are three persons in God. The three persons are God the Father, God the Son, and God the Holy Spirit.

God the Son wanted to come from heaven and live with us. He wanted to open heaven, so we could live there and see God. He wanted to show us how good and kind God is. He wanted to teach us how to be good, so we will be a little like God.

I believe...
in Jesus Christ, His only Son, Our Lord, who was conceived by the Holy Spirit, born of the Virgin Mary.

And God the Son became a little baby. His name was Jesus Christ. He was born in Bethlehem. The Holy Spirit gave Him the Virgin Mary to be His mother. Mary took care of Jesus until He grew up.

I believe...
in Jesus Christ, His only Son, Our Lord,
who was conceived by the Holy Spirit,
born of the Virgin Mary,
suffered under Pontius Pilate.

When Jesus was a grown man, He went around doing good to everybody. He showed people how to love God and get to heaven. He cured the sick and even made dead people live again.

Some bad men hated Jesus. They wanted to kill Him. Pontius Pilate, the governor, wanted to please them. He said, "Jesus hasn't done anything wrong. Kill Him if you want to, but don't bother me."

I believe...
in Jesus Christ, His only Son, Our Lord,
who was conceived by the Holy Spirit,
born of the Virgin Mary,
suffered under Pontius Pilate,
was crucified, died.

The bad men nailed Jesus to a cross and let Him die. Jesus chose to die, because that was the way He opened heaven for us. He loved us, and He loved everybody in the whole world. He wanted everybody to live in heaven with Him forever.

INRI

I believe...
in Jesus Christ, His only Son, Our Lord,
who was conceived by the Holy Spirit,
born of the Virgin Mary,
suffered under Pontius Pilate,
was crucified, died and was buried.

Mary, the mother of Jesus, stood by the cross and cried. The bad men would not let her help Him. When Jesus was dead, some good men helped take Him down from the cross. They went with Mary and laid His dead body in a cave. They put a big rock in front of the door to the cave and went home. They were very sad.

He descended into hell.

Heaven had been shut ever since Adam and Eve had sinned. Many good people had died. But they could not get into heaven. They had been waiting a long time, in a place which is called Sheol, or hell, although it is not the same hell where the devils live. As soon as Jesus died, His soul went down and told all the good people that He had made up for Adam's sin. Soon they would go to heaven with Him. How happy they were!

I believe…
the third day He rose again
from the dead.

Three days after Jesus died, He came back to life. He visited His Mother Mary and all His friends. How happy they were!

I believe...
He ascended into heaven.

Jesus stayed with his friends a while. He told them all about the holy Church He was going to start. He told them to go out and tell everybody in the world about Him. He wanted everybody to belong to His Church. When Jesus had finished teaching His friends, He went up to heaven.

I believe...
He ascended into heaven,
and sits at the right hand of God,
the Father Almighty.

In heaven, Jesus sits beside God, His Father. He waits for us to come and live with Him in heaven. He has built beautiful houses there for us to live in.

I believe...
From there He shall come to judge the living and the dead.

Someday Jesus will come again, and all people shall see Him in the sky. The dead will come to life again. We all will stand before Jesus. His clear bright eyes always see whether we have been good or bad. He will take the good people into heaven to live with God and the bad people will have to go to hell.

I believe in the Holy Spirit.

God the Father made the world and all of us. God the Son became Man and died on the cross to save us. God the Holy Spirit came to us when we were baptized. He makes our souls holy. Spirit means breath or wind. We cannot see the wind, but we know when it is blowing. We cannot see the Holy Spirit. Sometimes we draw His picture as a white dove. But the Holy Spirit is not a dove. He is God. The Holy Spirit lives in us when we are good.

I believe in …
the Holy Catholic Church.

Jesus started His Church to help us be good. The Holy Spirit takes care of the Church and makes it holy. Jesus stays with His Church all the time, because He loves us and wants to be near us. At Holy Mass we are present again on Calvary, where Jesus gives Himself to His Father to open heaven and make up for our sins. At Holy Communion Jesus comes to be one with us in our hearts.

I believe in ...
the communion of Saints.

Some people who die are good, but not quite good enough to go to heaven right away. They go to a place called purgatory, where they wait until their souls are worthy to enter heaven. We can pray for these people; they can pray for us. Besides this, the saints in heaven pray for us all. All the people of God's Church are like a great body. With Jesus as our head, we make up what is called "The Mystical Body of Christ."

I believe in...
the forgiveness of sins.

Jesus made up for all our sins when He died on the cross. He wanted our souls to be beautiful and clean. And He made it easy for us to keep them clean. Jesus gave His priests the power to wash our souls clean and white. But we must be sorry for our sins and promise not to disappoint Jesus again. At confession, we can think we see Jesus sitting there in the priest's place.

I believe in...
the resurrection of the body
and life everlasting.

Everybody must die someday. Jesus died because He wanted to make up for the sin of Adam and for our sins. Jesus came back to life again, to show us that we, too, will come back to life. When He comes to us in Holy Communion it is a promise that we, too, will live forever.

We will be bright and beautiful, like Jesus. We will never again be sad or sick or hurt, and we will never die any more. We will be with God and the angels in heaven forever.

This prayer is called The Apostles' Creed. The Apostles were the friends of Jesus. They wanted us all to know just what Jesus taught them, so they wrote down the Apostles' Creed for us.

THE APOSTLES' CREED

I believe in God the Father Almighty, Creator of heaven and earth, and in Jesus Christ, His only Son, our Lord, who was conceived by the Holy Spirit, born of the Virgin Mary, suffered under Pontius Pilate, was crucified, died, and was buried. He descended into hell; on the third day He rose again from the dead. He ascended into heaven, and is seated at the right hand of God, the Father Almighty; from there He shall come to judge the living and the dead. I believe in the Holy Spirit, the Holy Catholic Church, the communion of saints, the forgiveness of sins, the resurrection of the body and life everlasting. Amen.

IHS
I
II
III
IV
V
VI
VII
VIII
IX
X

IHS

I
II
III
IV
V
VI
VII
VIII
IX
X